FRYE'S PRACTICAL CANDY MAKER

LECTOR HOUSE PUBLIC DOMAIN WORKS

FRYE'S PRACTICAL CANDY MAKER

GEORGE V. FRYE

ISBN: 978-93-5344-893-6

Published: -

LECTOR HOUSE LLP
E-MAIL: lectorpublishing@gmail.com

FRYE'S PRACTICAL CANDY MAKER

COMPRISING PRACTICAL RECEIPTS FOR THE MANUFACTURE OF FINE "HAND-MADE" CANDIES, ESPECIALLY ADAPTED FOR FINE RETAIL TRADE.

BY

G. V. FRYE,

Practical Candy Maker,
Chicago, Ill.

PREFACE.

It is not my intention in presenting this volume to the trade to write a long, dry dissertation on Confectionery, but to give plain practical receipts for the manufacture of fine Hand-made Counter Goods, and as I make no pretensions to literary merit, I hope to disarm criticism.

The work is the fruit of years of personal experience in the manufacture of fine candies, and though containing much, it does not pretend to teach all that a candy-maker should know; that must be learned by years of practice. Although not perfect, confectioners will find this little volume a useful one, if not invaluable. Its utility even to those who are skilled in the art of candy making appears to the writer to be great. But it is more especially designed for confectioners whose business does not justify their securing the services of skilled workmen. Many confectioners would be glad to exhibit to their customers a fine display of choice hand-made candies, knowing that by so doing they would soon increase their trade, but the wages of a good workman, in this line, are high, and he can not afford to keep one. The prices asked for the goods, by those that will wholesale them, make them too expensive to be practical, and at the same time the goods do not ship in good order, even if he had a favorable opportunity of buying them, so he is obliged to handle a line of cheap goods, which seldom give any satisfaction, or at least, do not create a desire for candies from his place; hence, his trade, or what should be his trade, is swallowed up by those whose goods are fresh and tempting. To such, the importance of this little volume, ready at call, to assist the confectioner in making a fine line of counter goods, is too plain to require discussion.

In conclusion, I earnestly hope these practical receipts will be an acceptable offering to a very large number of confectioners, whose prosperity I would promote. To them it is commended with the respects of the author.

G. V. FRYE.

CONTENTS

BUTTER CUPS.

COCOANUT GOODS.

ALMOND GOODS.

MISCELLANEOUS GOODS.

CREAM GOODS.

SUGAR.

HOW TO SELECT

In selecting Sugar the confectioner must bear in mind that it is the foundation of all confectionery, and he can not expect to manufacture first-class goods except from first-class material; hence, select only Sugar that is perfectly dry and of uniform quality, and in white, hard, sparkling crystals; only such Sugar will give satisfaction.

In addition to selecting Sugar, particular attention must be paid to the changes that Sugar undergoes in passing from one degree to another while cooking, and also its action when united with such ingredients as cream of tartar, glucose, molasses, nuts, fruits, etc. This must be done if one expects to be a proficient workman in the art of making fine candies.

FACTS FOR THE WORKMAN.

To have the following receipts produce the results desired certain conditions are imposed on the workman. In the first place, the best of Confectioner's Sugar must be used. Second, one quart of water to each six pounds of sugar, unless more than eighteen pounds is used, in which case, add only one pint of water to each additional six pounds. Third, the amount of cream of tartar or glucose mentioned in each receipt. Fourth, that all goods are to be cooked over a rapid fire unless otherwise ordered. To show the importance of this I will illustrate: In several places I have said "cook the sugar until it begins to turn yellow or about 330° by the thermometer." Now, if the best sugar, right amount of cream of tartar and water, and the batch is boiled over a rapid fire, it will not vary but a degree or so from turning at 330°, but if a lower grade of sugar is used, more cream of tartar, more water, and the batch is boiled over a slow fire, the sugar will turn probably before the batch reaches 300°, and the goods when made would soon become sticky and unfit for the counter. There are often times when a poorer grade of sugar must be worked and there is no reason why poor goods should be made from it, but good judgment is necessary. If the sugar is damp, use only water enough to dissolve it, use less cream of tartar and cook over a very rapid fire; yet, such sugar can not be used for first-class goods, and should not be used at all unless the best can not be procured.

In flavoring candies never use ether flavors, only pure fruit extracts and oils.

Put all hard sugar goods, as soon as made, into air tight tin boxes, so they are not exposed to the atmosphere until needed for the counter.

In coloring the cheaper grades of hard candies, always make decided colors, but in the finer hard goods and cream work make only delicate shades.

Always dissolve cream of tartar in a small quantity of water before adding it to the batch

DEGREES OF BOILING, EITHER WITH THERMOMETER, SACCHAROMETER, OR WATER COOK,

THREAD.

The first degree found in boiling Sugar is called the Thread. The manner of ascertaining this is: having placed the batch on the furnace, which for example we will call six pounds of sugar and one quart of water, stir with a wooden spatula or skimming ladle until dissolved, having boiled a short time, raise the skimmer from the batch, pass the fore finger of the left hand across it, retaining on the end of the finger some of the syrup; now place the end of the finger on the thumb, and separate them, if a thread is formed between them, which breaks and settles on the thumb, the degree is reached. By the thermometer this degree is 220, by saccharometer 33°.

PEARL.

The next degree is the Pearl, and is indicated by trying as before, and if able to separate finger and thumb to fullest extent, the degree is reached. The thermometer will show at this degree, 226°, saccharometer, 37°.

BLOW.

Continue the boiling, and raising the skimmer, blow through it, if small air bubbles appear on opposite side, the blow is reached, and the thermometer will show 230°, saccharometer, 40°.

FEATHER.

Proceed with the boiling a few minutes, raise the skimmer and blow through it as before, if a greater number of air bubbles appear the degree is reached. The thermometer will indicate 236°, saccharometer, 42°.

SOFT BALL.

The next degree is the Soft Ball, and is determined in the following manner: Place a measure of cold water near the furnace, and after inserting the right hand in the water reach in the batch with two fore fingers and bring out a small portion of syrup, immediately putting your hand back in the water, and if you can work the syrup into a soft ball in the water it has reached that degree. The thermometer showing 240°, saccharometer, 44°.

HARD BALL.

In a short time try as before, and if you can form the syrup into a hard ball that will stick to the teeth, when bitten, the degree is reached. The thermometer show-ing 248°, the saccharometer after this degree ceases to indicate correctly.

SOFT CRACK.

The next degree reached, after continuing the boiling for a short time, is the Soft Crack. Try in the water, as before, and if the syrup cracks when pressed by the finger and thumb, but on holding a moment, forms into a hard ball again, it is the degree sought. The thermometer shows this degree to be 252°.

CRACK.

Test as before, and if the syrup cracks easily and will not form a ball, it has reached the crack. The thermometer marks this degree 260.

HARD CRACK.

The next degree we use, is when after being tested as before, it cracks like egg shells, and will eat up readily. The thermometer shows at this degree 290°.

The degrees higher than the Hard Crack or 290° are used only for such goods as machine drops, stick candies, etc., and will be explained as we proceed.

COLORS.

KINDS TO USE, AND HOW TO MAKE

In choosing Colors for candy, certain qualifications are necessary. First, they must not fade or change when exposed to the light. Second, they must not be easily affected by acids or alkalies; hence, it has been difficult to produce colors that are reasonably permanent and at the same time harmless. Yet the following will be found as near perfect as any yet produced.

RED, COCHINEAL COLOR.

Put on the fire, in a copper basin, two quarts of water; when it comes to a boil, add one fourth of a pound powdered Alum; then the same amount of powdered Cochineal; next, the same quantity of Salts of Tartar; let it boil a minute, stirring all the time, then set off the fire, and stir in six ounces Cream of Tartar; place again on the fire, and boil about five minutes; then strain through a fine sieve; when cool enough, put into a glass jar. Do not cover it, as it keeps much better when open to the air.

CARMINE.

Take a three or four ounce bottle, fill half full of best No. 40 Carmine, and add Ammonia sufficient to fill the bottle; shake well, and it is ready for use.

YELLOW, SAFFRON COLOR.

Put into a basin one pint of water, add to it two ounces of Spanish Saffron, twelve ounces of Sugar, and one ounce of powdered Alum, boil these together for eight or ten minutes, then strain through a damp flannel bag; when cold add to it one gill of Spirits of Wine, and bottle for use.

ANOTHER YELLOW.

This is made in the same way as the above, except use Fustic, instead of Saffron, and one quart of water; it comes cheaper, but when used with powdered sugar often turns brown, as much of the powdered sugar contains traces of iron, being ground in iron mills; but used with other goods it produces a bright yellow.

ORANGE.

This is made by adding red color to the yellow, and is done, as you need it, by simply coloring, whatever you want orange, a bright yellow, then add to it a few drops of red.

GREEN.

Take one peck of fresh Spinach, rub it to a pulp in a mortar, squeeze from it all juice possible, and put it in a basin on the fire, and it will soon curdle, as milk does when sour; immediately set off and strain through a fine sieve; take the curd and add to it its bulk in powdered Sugar, a few drops of Spirits of Wine, and what powdered Alum you can hold on the point of a pen knife; bottle for use. Another nice green can be made by adding to the second formula given for making yellow, a sufficient quantity of Indigo to make it the shade desired.

BLUE.

Powder one-half ounce of Indigo, add to it enough Simple Syrup to make it the consistency of cream, and one-half ounce Spirits of Wine.

BURNT SUGAR COLOR.

Take any quantity of scrap, dissolve and strain them, set on the fire and cook until it begins to burn; now deaden the fire a little and let burn slowly until very black, and the syrup, when raising the spatula, does not run off freely; then add, very slowly, two gallons of boiling water to each ten pounds of syrup, cooked by means of a long handled dipper, pouring a stream no larger than a straw at first, when all is added; let boil a few moments, then put into a crock for use.

STICK CANDIES.

As this line of goods are sold so cheap, the manufacturer of it is almost entirely confined to the wholesale factory, the retailer preferring to buy rather than to make it; yet, for those who may wish to make their own, below will be found a formula which will make first-class goods, but it must be remembered that considerable practice and good taste is necessary to make nice stick candy.

PEPPERMINT STICK.

Twelve pounds of sugar, two quarts of water, stir until dissolved, then add one full teaspoon of cream of tartar, (or if you wish to use glucose, add three pounds of same, do this when you are weighing your sugar, by hollowing out a place in the center of the sugar and pouring in the glucose). Now put on the steamer and let it remain until the batch begins to cook, then remove; in this way all the grains of sugar adhereing to the sides of the basin are washed down; however, if any should remain they must be removed with a damp sponge or cloth, as otherwise they might grain your batch. Now cook till the sugar just begins to turn yellow, then remove at once and pour out on a greased slab, or if boiling by a thermometer, remove batch at about 330°. Now throw in the edges of the batch and fold all together, take about two pounds of the batch while it is still hot, and add to it red color, and work it in with your hands or a batch knife, then place it on the spinning table before the heater, to keep it warm. Now place the batch on the hook, and flavor with peppermint oil, and pull perfectly white, then form it into a roll; take about one-half of the red piece and pull it into a wide strip just long enough to reach lengthwise across the batch, then spin out the remainder of the red into six small strips, and place them in same manner on batch, about one inch apart; then taking hold of one end of the batch with right hand, hold it up, letting it form itself into the shape of a wine bottle; now roll it before the heater until it is warm enough to spin out nicely, and while one person keeps the batch in shape, let another spin it out, rolling it as he does so; when of the length desired break it off by suddenly striking it with the edge of the hand, or cutting with the shears, and have a third party roll until cold, then cut the sticks in lengths wanted, by means of the candy shears.

LEMON STICK.

Prepare and cook same as peppermint; leave the batch clear, and flavor with Lemon Oil on the slab before throwing it together; then takeing about, or a little more than half the quantity that you colored red for mint, pull white on the hook;

form this into strips on the batch, as you did in mint, then spin out somewhat smaller, as the candy being clear will weigh heavier.

WINTERGREEN STICK.

Same as before, except when it begins to boil, color red in the basin; when poured out on the slab and cooled enough to pull, reserve about one pound of the clear red for the stripes; then having pulled the remainder a nice pink shade, form the clear red piece into three stripes, of even size, and place them on the batch about three inches apart, and proceed as before.

CINNAMON STICK.

Same as peppermint, except put three red stripes, as in wintergreen.

SASSAFRAS STICK.

Pulled white, with two red and one yellow stripe, the yellow being between the red.

CLOVE STICK.

Clear, with three white stripes of even size.

FRUIT ROCK.

These goods require a great deal of practice, and a new beginner will waste considerable sugar before he can accomplish it in first-class style. I shall explain a few kinds, and by the time you can make these nicely you will be able to make any design you may wish.

STRAWBERRY ROCK.

Boil any amount of sugar, treat in the same manner as for stick candy; when done pour out almost two-thirds of batch on the slab, and color the rest red in the basin, and place again on the furnace, stirring the color into the batch, then pour out. Now take a small piece of the first poured out, say three-fourths of a pound, and color green and place it before the heater. Now pull the remaining perfectly white; take about one pound of this and form into a roll, about four or five inches in length, then wrap around this about one-third of your red batch. Now spin this out about five feet in length, and cut it into fifteen pieces about four inches in length. Now put five of these together, then four on top of these, then three, then two and one, forming a triangle. Now form your green into a very thin, wide strip about twelve inches in length; cut in three equal pieces, lay two of these flat on the table and stand the third one in the middle. Now place a block of white on either side of the perpendicular piece, forming a square of the whole; place this on the base of the triangle already formed. Now wrap all the white remaining around the whole, then forming the red into a thin sheet wrap around the white and spin out as stick candy, when cold cut into small cuts, by holding a stick in the left hand, letting it rest on an iron bar and cutting with a knife in the right.

LEMON SLICES.

Having cooked your batch same as last, pour all out on the slab and color one-fourth yellow; pull another one-fourth white, take of the white just pulled one-half pound and roll all the clear around it in such a way as the white will be in the center, then cut this into two pieces, one being somewhat larger than the other; take the larger one, spin it out into a strip about three feet in length, and cut into six sticks of even length; place two of these together and third one on top, forming a triangle; do the same with the other three, cut a small piece from the pulled piece left and form it into two thin sheets and cover two sides of the two triangles; pull out the remaining clear piece same as the other and form two more triangles; then place the two triangles covered white opposite each other, then the two other ones opposite, the sharp edges of all meeting in the center. Now wrap the white remaining around this, then the yellow, and spin out as before.

CHECKERBOARD.

Having poured the batch on the slab, color one-third of it chocolate; this is done by kneeding into the batch about one and one-half ounces of melted chocolate to each pound. Now leave another one-third of the batch clear and pull the remaining third, reserving from it before pulling, one and one-half pounds; form the clear into a square, also the chocolate and place both together, then pull it out eight feet in length, keeping the strips square. Now cut into sixteen pieces of six inches each and build into a square block, the chocolate on the clear, the clear on the chocolate, then wrap the white around it and spin out the small clear piece into very small strips and place them on the batch about one inch apart, proceed to spin out as before.

LETTERED CANDY.

This is made in the same manner as the Fruit Rock, and simply requires good taste and practice.

COUGH, AND OTHER DROPS.

LEMON OR SOUR DROPS.

Cook your batch the same as for Lemon Stick, about twelve pounds, pour it out on the slab, fill an ordinary glass half full of tartaric acid, add a little water, and work it into a paste; scatter this over the batch, also a few drops of lemon oil. Now throw the batch together, and with the batch knife work the acid through the batch; when cold enough run through the drop machine, any design desired; remember the acid and flavor must be worked in while the batch is still hot. The old way of using the acid, dry, does not make as nice drop as the paste.

MINT DROPS.

Take twelve pounds of sugar, treat it in the same manner as you would for Mint Stick. Color about two pounds red, for the stripes, pull the rest white, form it into a roll and place fine red stripes around the batch, about one inch apart; spin out as stick candy, but do not roll it, as the stripes should remain straight; run through a sour drop cutter.

"OLD STYLE" MINT DROPS.

Cook any number of pounds of clear scraps, as high as possible without burning; use no cream of tartar or glucose; pour on the slab and flavor with mint oil before throwing together, pull a small piece of the batch as white as possible, and form it into stripes about one inch apart, around the batch, and run through a drop machine.

MALT DROPS.

Twelve pounds of Sugar, small spoon of cream tartar or two pounds of glucose, and cook until sugar begins to turn, or about 330° by the thermometer, if using cream of tartar; if glucose, the sugar will turn sooner. Now add about one pint extract of Malt, slowly; this should be warm before adding, stir until batch is ready to pour on the slab, which will require a few moments, as the Malt reduces the batch; be very careful and not let it scorch or burn, as that will destroy the fine flavor of the Malt; run through a drop machine, any design wished.

LIME JUICE DROPS.

Twelve pounds of Sugar, small spoon of cream of tartar, or three pounds of glucose; cook until sugar is just on the point of turning yellow, keeping the sides of the basin well washed down; pour out at once on oiled or greased slab, add to batch about one-half as much tartaric acid as for Lemon Drops; form the acid into a paste by adding to it a few drops of Lime Juice, work it into the batch, in the same way as for lemon, together with half a teaspoon green color, and a few drops of Oil of Lime; then run through a drop machine, forming a thin round, or square drop.

WILD CHERRY DROPS.

Twelve pounds of Sugar, small spoon of cream of tartar, or three pounds of glucose; when it boils add a few drops of red color, just enough to tint the batch, then cook to a very Hard Crack, or 300° or 310°. Set off and stir in a tablespoon of extract of Wild Cherry and pour out on a greased slab between iron bars. Make the batch cover a space at least three feet square; as soon as it cools a little, run over it with a caramel marker, both ways; this must be done quickly or the batch will get too cold to mark.

HOARHOUND DROPS.

Boil in three quarts of water for five or ten minutes about five ounces of Hoarhound, then strain through a fine sieve. Take this liquor and add to it twelve pounds of Sugar and a small spoon of cream of tartar, or two pounds of glucose, and cook to a Hard Crack, or 290° or 300°. Then pour out and run through a machine, or mark with a caramel marker, as Wild Cherry. All or part clear scraps can be used instead of sugar, in which case use no cream of tartar or glucose.

BONESET DROPS.

Same as Hoarhound, except make a liquor of Boneset instead of Hoarhound.

ICELAND MOSS DROPS.

Boil five ounces of Iceland Moss in three quarts of water for ten minutes; strain and add to liquor twelve pounds of Sugar, small spoon cream of tartar, or two pounds glucose; when it comes to a boil color a deep red; cook to same degree as Hoarhound, flavor with a few drops Oil Anise and pour on slab between iron bars and mark with caramel marker.

FLAX SEED DROPS.

Six pounds of Sugar, one quart of water, small spoon of cream of tartar, or one or two pounds of glucose; cook to a Hard Crack, then stir in three ounces of whole or powdered Flax-seeds and let cook a few moments; pour out and either mark into squares with caramel marker, or run through a drop machine.

ENGLISH BARLEY SUGAR DROPS.

Six pounds of Sugar, small spoon cream of tartar, or one pound of glucose; cook to a Hard Crack, or 290°. Stir in four ounces butter and a few drops of Lemon

Oil, then pour out and mark as Iceland Moss, etc.

TAR DROPS.

Six pounds of Sugar, small spoon of cream of tartar, or two pounds of glucose; cook to a Hard Crack, or 290°. Pour out on a well greased slab and add about a small spoon of Pine Tar; then with a batch knife work it through the batch, and run through a drop machine.

FRUIT DROPS, FIVE FLAVORS.

Twenty pounds of Sugar, three quarts of water, a heaping teaspoon of cream of tartar, or sixteen pounds of Sugar and four pounds of glucose; cook till the Sugar begins to turn yellow, then pour out at once; to one fourth of the batch add two or three drops of red color, just enough to make it a bright pink, then two full teaspoons of tartaric acid paste, and a few drops of Nectar; to another fourth of the batch add sufficient red color to make it a deep red, the same quantity of acid paste, and a few drops of Strawberry flavor; to the remaining half of the batch add as much acid as was given to the other two and a few drops of Lemon Oil; run these through a drop machine, forming round drops. Now cook ten pounds of Sugar in the same manner, color one-half of it Orange shade and flavor, add acid paste as before, the other half color green, and flavor Lime Juice; run through the same set of rolls.

TAFFIES.

VANILLA TAFFY.

Six pounds of Sugar, small spoon of cream of tartar or two pounds of glucose; cook just to the Crack, or 252°, add to it while cooking one Vanilla Bean, split in two; when poured on the slab remove the bean, and when cold enough, pull perfectly white; remove from the hook and pull into long strips, then cut into pieces three or four inches in length, and wrap in wax paper. If brittle taffy is wanted, cook this same batch to the Hard Crack, or 290°; form it into a large cake, which may be broken with a hammer as sold. If flavoring with the extract instead of the bean, do so while pulling on the hook.

PINE APPLE TAFFY.

Cook same as Vanilla, except add no flavor in basin, and let the batch reach the Hard Crack degree, then pour out two-thirds of the batch; color the rest in the basin a bright red, pull the first poured out, white, and flavor Pine Apple; form it into a cake, and having spread the red pieces out into a sheet, cover it over the white.

LEMON TAFFY.

Same as Vanilla; color yellow in the basin before pouring out, then flavor Lemon on the hook.

CHOCOLATE TAFFY.

Same as Vanilla; when on the slab add to the batch six ounces melted Chocolate, work it into the batch with a batch knife.

COCOANUT TAFFY.

Six pounds of Sugar, small spoon of cream of tartar, or three pounds of glucose; cook to the Hard Crack, then add three grated Cocoanuts; stir until the batch reaches the Soft Crack; pour out at once; when sufficiently cold, pull white on the hook, and run out into strips; cut into pieces, any length desired, and wrap in wax paper.

"OLD STYLE" MOLASSES.

Five pounds of Sugar and one gallon of N. O. Molasses; put on the fire and cook to a Hard Ball, then add two pounds of sweet butter, and continue the cooking until the batch just reaches the Soft Crack, or 252°, if in winter; if in summer, cook to the Crack, or 260°; pour out on a greased slab, and pull to a bright golden color; form into strips, and cut into bars four or five inches in length; wrap in wax paper.

ANOTHER MOLASSES TAFFY.

Three pounds of Sugar, three pounds of glucose, and one quart of Molasses; cook to the Soft Crack; set off and stir into the batch one teaspoon of saleratus; pour on a slab, and when nearly cold pull and flavor on the hook, either with a few drops of Lemon Oil, Bitter Almond Oil, or Extract of Mace; run out into bars as before.

TAFFIES, (EXTRA FINE).

HICKORY-NUT TAFFY.

Six pounds of Sugar, and just enough Molasses to color; a small spoon of cream of tartar, or four pounds of Sugar and two of glucose; cook to the Hard Crack; pour out on a greased slab, and before throwing together, scatter over it about two pounds of chopped up Hickory-nuts; work the nuts into the batch, then run it through a flake machine, about two inches wide, and mark with a caramel marker into sticks. These are very nice goods for fancy boxes.

WALNUT TAFFY.

Same as Hickory Nut, with the exception of the nuts.

COCOANUT TAFFY.

Same as others, except add three grated Cocoanuts, when batch has reached the Hard Crack, and stir until the batch again reaches the same degree; run through the flake machine, as wide as the machine will admit, then mark with a caramel marker, diagonally, two ways, forming diamonds. These are very handsome.

BRAZIL-NUT TAFFY.

Same as Walnut or Hickory-nut; but use no molasses, and when done, set off and stir in one teaspoon saleratus; mark into sticks.

BAR CANDIES.

BROWN ALMOND BAR.

Ten pounds of Sugar, large spoon of cream of tartar, and when it begins to boil, add six pounds of Almond Nuts, after having picked out all shells and dusted the nuts thoroughly; stir slowly, keeping the sides of the basin well washed, until nuts are as brown as wished, and slide off the spatula easily when raised up; pour out between iron bars, about one inch thick; when cold enough not to run, cut into bars with batch knife and a mallet.

BROWN ALMOND BAR, (WITH GLUCOSE).

Six pounds of Sugar, four pounds of glucose; cook to the Hard Crack, then add six pounds of Almond Nuts; stir until the nuts cease cracking, and it is done; pour out as before.

BLANCHED ALMOND BAR.

Same as Brown Almond, except blanch the Almonds; this should be done sometime before making the bar, so the nuts will be dry.

PEA-NUT BAR.

Same as Almond Bar, except use ten pounds of Pea-nuts.

SLICED COCOANUT.

Ten pounds of Sugar, large spoon of cream of tartar; cook to a Hard Crack, or 290°, then add slowly, five sliced Cocoanuts; (after paring the Cocoanuts, cut them into halves, then slice them with a spoke shave); stir carefully, till nuts are as brown as desired, then pour out between iron bars, same as other nut bars. If cooking with glucose, use same quantity as for Almond Bar.

BRAZIL BAR.

Ten pounds of Sugar, ordinary spoon of cream of tartar, or six pounds of Sugar and four pounds of glucose; cook to a Hard Crack, or 290°, then pour out one-half of the batch between iron bars, and scatter over this five or six pounds of Brazil-nuts, after trimming all the dark skin off them so that they are nice and white; now pour over the nuts the remaining syrup, and cut into bars.

ENGLISH WALNUT BAR.

Same as Brazil-nut Bar.

FRUIT CANDY.

Six pounds of Sugar, one quart of water, a heaping spoon of cream of tartar, or two pounds of glucose; cook to a Hard Crack; then add, carefully, four pounds of fruit, such as Cherries, Figs, seeded Dates, cut up Citron, blanched Almonds, Brazil-nuts, a few slices of Cocoanut, or any other nice fruits or nuts; stir slowly, for a few minutes, until the fruits slide off the spatula, freely; then pour out on a greased slab between iron bars, and cut into bars as Nut Candy.

MOLASSES SLICED COCOANUT.

Open, pare and slice, with a spoke shave, five fresh Cocoanuts; then place on a slow fire, one quart best N. O. Molasses, and one-fourth pound sweet Butter; when it boils add the Cocoanuts; stir all the time over a very slow fire until it reaches the Soft Crack, in winter, or Crack, in summer; pour out on a greased slab, and spread out thin with a palette knife, then cut into such sized bars as wished; wrap in wax paper in summer.

BLACK WALNUT CANDY.

Six pounds of Sugar, one quart of water, small spoon of cream of tartar, or one pound of glucose, and one-half pint N. O. Molasses; cook to a Hard Crack, then add one-half pound sweet Butter, and stir until the batch again reaches the Hard Crack; set off and stir in one teaspoon saleratus; then pour out on a greased slab, and scatter over the batch two pounds of picked-over Walnuts; fold up the batch and kneed the Walnuts through it; then, when cold enough, form into a small square; lay before the heater on the spinning table, and while one person keeps it in shape, let another cut it into slices. Another way is to cook just to the Soft Crack, and serve in the same manner as above, but wrap the squares in wax paper.

CARAMELS.

These Caramel receipts are the *best in the world*, and the author questions the ability of any one to produce a Caramel that will excell them in any particular. After once making by either one of the following formulas, no other will be used, as they are worth a dozen times the price of this book, to any one wishing to give his trade a fine Caramel.

VANILLA CARAMELS, NO. 1.

Open eight cans of Condensed Milk, (Osprey Brand, is the best, manufactured by Canfield Condensed Milk Co., Baltimore, Md.; when this can not be procured, use Eagle Brand); empty cans into one gallon of sweet Cream, and stir until all is of one consistency; reject all small lumps that may be in the milk, as they will settle at the bottom, and burn the batch; now add to the mixture twelve pounds of Sugar and six pounds of glucose; put on the fire, and when it begins to boil, split three Vanilla Beans to the stem, and scrape out the centers; tie the beans together at one end, and add them, with the scrapings, to the batch; cook over a slow fire, to a Soft Crack, stirring all the time; pour out and remove the beans. In case the extract of Vanilla is used, add it just before pouring out on the slab.

VANILLA CARAMELS, NO. 2.

Twelve pounds of Sugar, six quarts of good Cream, two Vanilla Beans, and one pound of sweet Butter; cook over a rapid fire to a good Crack; put the Sugar, two quarts of the cream and the beans on the fire; when it boils, add two quarts more of the cream; when it again reaches a boil, add the remaining two quarts; then, as it again comes to a boil, add two heaping spoons of cream of tartar.

MAPLE CARAMELS.

Use six pounds of A Sugar, six pounds of Maple Sugar, and six pounds of glucose; then proceed as for Vanilla, with the exception of the flavor.

STRAWBERRY CARAMELS.

Same as Vanilla No. 2; color red in the basin, and flavor before pouring out, with the extract of Strawberry.

COCOANUT CARAMELS.

Same as Vanilla; if cooking according to Vanilla No. 1, (as I always recommend,) add three grated Cocoanuts, when the batch has reached the Hard Ball. If by Vanilla No. 2, add the Cocoanuts at first, with the sugar and cream, using a little more cream of tartar than for Vanilla.

HONEY CARAMELS.

Same as Vanilla, except use six pounds of Sugar, six of Honey, and six of glucose.

PULLED CARAMELS.

Cook six pounds of Sugar and six pounds of glucose with six quarts of Cream and one-half pound of sweet butter to a Soft Crack; pour out on the slab, and when nearly cold, place on the hook and pull as white as possible, then form into a thin sheet on a slab and roll with a rolling-pin until of even thickness; mark and cut as other Caramels.

CHOCOLATE CARAMELS.

Use seven cans of Condensed Milk with one gallon of Cream; after mixing it, reserve one quart and add to the rest twelve pounds of Sugar, six pounds of glucose, and two Vanilla Beans; cook over a slow fire till about half done; then set off; break up one and a fourth pounds of Chocolate; put it into a basin with a little water; put on the fire, and when hot, add the one quart of Cream, a little at a time, until the Chocolate is dissolved; strain it into the batch; then set on the fire again, and cook to a Soft Crack.

CHOCOLATE CREAM CARAMELS.

Make a batch same as last, but only one-half the size; pour it out on the slab very thin; prepare about six pounds of cream by working very smooth, then with a rolling-pin roll it into a thin sheet, and spread it over one-half the batch; fold the other half of the batch over this and press it well down; mark with Caramel marker, and cut as other Caramels.

OPERA CARAMELS—VANILLA.

Ten pounds of Sugar and one gallon of Cream, one Vanilla Bean split and scraped as before, one full spoon of cream tartar—add this after the batch has reached the boil; cook just to a Soft Ball, stirring all the time; pour out on a damp slab, made so by sprinkling on a very little water; when cold, cream it with a cream scraper, and after working it perfectly smooth, form the whole into a sheet about one-half inch thick, between iron bars and on wax paper; run the rolling-pin over it and mark with Caramel marker; after it remains on the slab an hour or so, cut into strips, three or four rows wide, and place in pans.

OPERA CARAMELS—MAPLE.

Same as Vanilla, excepting use five pounds of Maple Sugar and five pounds of

A Sugar, and a very small spoon cream tartar.

OPERA CARAMELS—CHOCOLATE.

Same as Vanilla, except reserve one quart of cream to dissolve one pound of Chocolate; strain this into the batch when half done; cook to a Soft Ball, and cream and shape as before.

NUT CARAMELS.

Cook same as Vanilla No. 1; add four pounds of Nuts, either Black Walnut, English Walnut, Hickory-nut or Brazil to the batch; when at a hard ball, or when the batch is done, pour out one-half between iron bars; scatter over it the Nuts, and cover them with what remains in the basin.

BUTTER CUPS.

Ten pounds of Sugar, two quarts of water; when it boils add one-half pint New Orleans Molasses and small spoon of cream tartar (or seven pounds of Sugar and three of glucose); cook to 310°; then add one pound of sweet Butter, and stir until dissolved; pour out on a greased slab; before cooking the above, take about five pounds of Vanilla Cream, work smooth and place before the heater on the spinning table; keep turning it and working the heat into it until it is quite hot; now put the above on the fire, and when poured out and cool as candy we intend to pull; spread it out into a sheet about one inch thick, twelve or fourteen inches wide, and sixteen in length; place the warm cream, having formed it into a roll, on the center of the batch lengthwise; now fold the covering over the cream making the edges meet; roll before the heater until warm, sufficient to work nicely; then spin out as stick candy, and mark with Caramel marker.

HICKORY-NUT CUPS.

Chop fine one and one-half pounds of Hickory-nuts; place them on the spinning table before the heater with four pounds of Cream; as the Cream gets warm, work the nuts through it; when all are worked in, put on ten pounds of Sugar and a small spoon of cream tartar; cook until Sugar just begins to turn, or about 330° by the thermometer; then pour out at once; when sufficiently cold, place on the hook and pull until it has a white satin appearance; then remove from the hook and form into shape as for Butter Cups; place the cream across the center and fold over the batch, making the edges meet; then spin out as before.

To make a center that will chew, cook two pounds of Sugar and three of glucose to a hard ball; pour on the slab, and work into it one and one-half pounds of chopped-up Hickory-nuts. One-fourth of a pound of sweet Butter, and one Vanilla Bean may be added, while cooking, if desired. A very nice center may be made by cooking one gallon best New Orleans Molasses to a hard ball, over a slow fire; pour out on the slab, and work in chopped-up Hickory-nuts, Walnuts, or Cream Nuts. Another popular center is made by running through a Cocoanut grater a quantity of fresh Figs, and then working into them powdered Sugar sufficient to form a smooth paste.

NECTAR CUPS.

Same as Hickory-nut Cups, except make a center of almond paste, colored light green; when on the slab, add to the clear batch a few drops of red color, some Nectar flavor, and fold all together, pull on the hook to a bright pink, and finish as before.

WALNUT CUPS.

Same as Hickory-nut Cups, with the exception of the Nuts.

COCOANUT CUPS.

Prepare a center by cooking two pounds of Sugar and three of glucose to a Crack, or 260°; add two grated Cocoanuts; stir a moment, and pour out on the slab; fold up and keep warm at the heater; put on the fire ten pounds of Sugar, small spoon of cream tartar, and cook until Sugar begins to turn; then add one-fourth of a pint of New Orleans Molasses; stir a moment, pour out and finish as before. You may use for center a small batch of Japanese Cocoanut cooked to a ball.

CHOCOLATE CUPS.

Use for a center five pounds of Vanilla Cream; cook a covering same as for Hickory-nut Cups; when on the slab, pour over the batch three-fourths of a pound melted Chocolate; fold together and work the Chocolate thoroughly through the batch; finish as before.

LEMON OR SOUR CUPS.

Make a center from five pounds of Sugar and a heaping spoon of cream tartar, or three pounds of glucose and three of Sugar; cook to a Hard Ball; when on the slab, add one-fourth of a tumbler of paste, made of tartaric acid (same as Lemon Drops); prepare the covering same as Hickory-nut Cups; color yellow; pull on the hook; flavor Oil Lemon and finish as before.

FRUIT CUPS.

Three pounds of Cream, two pounds of Fruits chopped up and mixed through the cream; these fruits should be chopped up sometime before using, so they may dry; prepare a covering as for Hickory-nut Cups, but do not pull it; this allows the fruit to show through the covering, and looks very handsome.

COCOANUT GOODS.

COCOANUT BAR, (WHITE).

Seven pounds of Sugar, one quart of Water; when it comes to a boil add six grated Cocoanuts, and stir until it reaches a good thread; set it off on a barrel and add a drop or two of blueing; now with the spatula, granulate the batch by working it on the sides of the basin, and stirring the whole batch until it becomes white; then pour out on a sugared slab; by this is meant, having arranged the iron bars to hold the batch; sieve over the inclosed surface pulverized Sugar, also over the tops of the bars; then turn the bars over carefully, so the sugared edge will be on the inside of the enclosure. In this space having poured the batch smooth it down with a palette knife, and let remain over night if possible; then cut into bars; use no flavor.

COCOANUT BAR (RED).

Same as White, except color Red in the basin before granulating it.

COCOANUT BAR (YELLOW).

Same as White, except color Yellow in the basin.

VANILLA COCOANUT PASTE.

Eight pounds of Sugar, two quarts of sweet Cream, one small spoon of cream tartar, one Vanilla Bean, and three grated Cocoanuts; cook to a soft ball, stirring all the time; pour out on a damp slab; when cold, cream it and mould in deep pans; let it remain for twelve hours or so, then cut into slices.

STRAWBERRY COCOANUT PASTE.

Same as Vanilla, except when creamed, color it Pink and flavor Strawberry.

MAPLE COCOANUT PASTE.

Five pounds of Maple Sugar, three pounds of A Sugar, small spoon cream tartar, and three grated Cocoanuts; proceed as for Vanilla.

CHOCOLATE COCOANUT PASTE.

Dissolve eight ounces of Chocolate in one quart of Cream; add this to eight pounds of Sugar, one quart of Cream, one Vanilla Bean, three grated Cocoanuts, and a heaping spoon of cream tartar; cook to a soft ball and finish as before.

WHITE COCOANUT CAKES.

Cook five pounds of Sugar with five Cocoanuts, grated in long strips, to a thread; set off the fire, and with the spatula granulate the batch until the body of the Sugar becomes cloudy; then place the basin on a barrel near the slab, having previously sugared the slab; take a tablespoon, dip a quantity of the Cocoanut from the basin; then by means of a stick, remove it from the spoon, dropping it on the slab; so continue until all is formed into cakes, or a small quantity may be reserved and colored red; then add a portion to each cake, placing it on the tops.

MOLASSES COCOANUT CAKES.

To five grated Cocoanuts, long cut, add one quart New Orleans Molasses; cook to a Hard Ball, over a very slow fire, and proceed as for white cakes, except drop them on a greased slab, and do not attempt to granulate the batch.

COCOANUT POTATOES.

Five pounds of Sugar, nearly a quart of water, small spoon of cream tartar; cook to 275°; then set off, and stir in two grated Cocoanuts; pour out on a damp slab and cream it; then roll out into a strip, one inch in diameter, and cut into pieces weighing two ounces; form these in the shape of potatoes, and roll them in ground cinnamon; then split some blanched Almonds into four strips each and stick them into the Potatoes, one at either end, and one on either side, resembling sprouts on Potatoes.

COCOANUT BISCUIT.

Take one and one-half pounds of powdered Sugar to each grated Cocoanut; put it into an earthern vessel, and work to a paste with the hands; use a little Orange Flower water, if desired; now, taking a tin tube, say six inches in length, one and one-half inches in diameter, having a rod with a head just fitting the tube; press the tube into the paste, having it of even thickness in a pan; then force the paste from the tube with the rod, forming a biscuit; when all are formed, take a fine, small brush and dip it in burnt Sugar color, and daub a little on the top of each biscuit, to give them the appearance of being browned in an oven; now, wrap them in wax paper, twisting both ends as in French kisses.

JAPANESE COCOANUT.

Five pounds of glucose, and two pounds of Sugar, one quart of water; when it comes to a boil, add five pounds of grated Cocoanut; cook to a Hard Ball, stirring all the time; pour out on a greased slab, between iron bars; make it of even thickness with a palette knife; when cold, mark diagonally two ways with Caramel marker, forming diamonds; then roll in pulverized Sugar, or crystalize them.

MOLASSES COCOANUT JAP.

Place on a slow fire two quarts of New Orleans Molasses, and one-half pound Butter; when it boils, add ten grated Cocoanuts, and stir until it reaches a hard ball; then pour out on a greased slab, between bars; spread thickness desired with a palette knife; when cold, cut into squares or diamonds.

SPANISH COCOANUT KISSES.

Grate six fresh Cocoanuts, then place on the fire eight pounds of Sugar, and just sufficient water to dissolve it; when it boils, add the Cocoanuts, and stir until it reaches a thread; set off and stir in a few drops blueing; now, pour into a lip basin a small portion, and with a small wooden spatula, granulate until it becomes cloudy; then drop on sheets of tin, cutting the drops from the lip pan by means of a wire; make the drops the size of a silver quarter.

ALMOND GOODS.

ALMOND PASTE.

Blanch four pounds of Almond-nuts; put them into a vessel and cover with water; let them stand for four or five hours; now, drain them; pound and rub them to a smooth paste in a mortar, adding a little Orange Flower water to keep them from oiling; when the paste is finished, put on the fire eight pounds of Sugar and cook to a crack; set off on a barrel and add the Almond paste; stir continually until the batch is cold, then put the paste into a crock for use.

ALMOND GEMS.

Ten pounds of Sugar, two quarts of water, small spoon of cream tartar; or seven pounds of Sugar and three pounds of glucose; add to batch one-half pint of New Orleans Molasses; stir till dissolved, then cook to 300°, and add one pound of sweet Butter; stir a moment, then pour out; scatter over the batch two pounds of chopped-up Almond-nuts; work all together, and run through a drop machine.

CREAM ALMONDS.

Pick over four pounds of Almond-nuts, rejecting all pieces and imperfect ones; cook sixteen pounds of Sugar and two quarts of water to a good ball; set it near the fire to keep warm; put the Almonds into a basin; set it over the fire, and stir the nuts around until quite hot; now, empty the nuts into a shaker-kettle, and while one person throws the nuts about by shaking the kettle, let another person pour the hot syrup, by means of a lip pan, over the Almonds in a thin, continuous stream; continue in this way until the nuts are as large as desired; if flavoring the syrup with Vanilla, leave the syrup clear; if with Rose or Nectar, color it with a few drops of red.

Another way to make Cream Almonds on a small scale, is to put into a sieve two pounds of selected Almonds; hold them over the fire, shaking them until very hot; cook eight pounds of Sugar to a good ball; use one-half spoon of cream tartar; when done, set near the fire; put the sieve containing the Almonds on the table, and while one person pours the hot syrup over the Almonds in a thin stream, let another person shake the sieve, letting it rest on the table. In making Jordan Cream Almonds, use only one and a half or two pounds of Sugar to each pound of Nuts.

BURNT ALMONDS.

Six pounds of Jordan Almonds, six pounds of Sugar and one quart of water, when the Sugar comes to a boil, add the nuts, and cook over a very slow fire until the nuts cease to crack; in this way, the nuts will be thoroughly roasted; now, set off the basin, and stir and turn the batch about until the Sugar granulates, throw all into a sieve, and shake the loose Sugar off; put this into the basin, with a little water to dissolve it; cook to a Soft Ball; remove the basin from the fire, and add the nuts; stir and turn the batch until the Sugar again granulates; throw into the sieve and shake off the loose Sugar as before; put it into the basin with enough Sugar added to make six pounds; add water to dissolve, and color a deep red; cook to a Soft Ball; remove and add Almonds as before; while granulating the Sugar this time, add one teaspoon of ground cinnamon; now, put into the basin one pint of dissolved gum arabic, made black by adding burnt Sugar color to it; set this on the fire, and when it boils, set off and throw in the Almonds; stir, throwing the nuts over and over until all are covered with the gum; then spread them out on a tray, and put in a warm place to dry; to make a hard coating, cook the Sugar to a Hard Crack, or 290° each time, instead of a soft ball; this kind will retain the gloss much longer, but the soft covering is the most popular.

SALTED ALMONDS.

Take any number pounds of blanched Almonds; put them into a pea-nut roaster, and roast them to a bright yellow color; throw them into a basin, and pour over them a little dissolved gum arabic; stir so all will be covered with it; now sprinkle over them table salt; remove them from the basin, and spread them out on a pan; they will soon be dry, with the salt adhering to them.

ALMOND NOUGAT.

Put into a copper basin two quarts of Honey, and the whites of two dozen Eggs; beat to a staunch foam; set on a very gentle fire, made so by covering it with ashes; now, with a long-handled egg-beater stir continually for two hours; when time is about up, cook eight pounds of Sugar with a large spoon of cream tartar to a Hard Crack, or 290°; then put the basin, containing the eggs and honey, on a barrel, and while one person stirs, let another pour in slowly the syrup just cooked; when thoroughly mixed, stir in about three pounds of Pistache nuts, or Pistache and blanched Almond nuts mixed, or all blanched Almonds, (the nuts must be well dried after blanching), then pour out into a starch tray, previously prepared, by lining it with ordinary paper; then again with wafer paper; spread the batch of even thickness with a palette knife; then cover the top with wafer paper, and set away to cool—this will require about ten or twelve hours in summer; when cold, cut with a sharp knife into pieces about three or four inches in length, and wrap in wax paper.

MISCELLANEOUS GOODS.

FRUIT CAKE.

Ten pounds of Sugar, two quarts of Cream, one spoon of cream tartar, or two pounds of glucose; cook to a Soft Ball, stirring all the time; pour on a damp slab, and when cold, cream it; then work into it three or four pounds of French Fruits; mold it in large cake pans, and set away a few hours to harden; cut it into slices as sold.

NUT CAKES.

Are made in the same way, except use Nuts instead of Fruit; Walnuts or Hickory-nuts are the best.

CREAM PEPPERMINTS.

Take of Cream, such as is prepared for dipping purposes, about three or four pounds; put this into a small basin inside of another basin containing hot water; stir until dissolved; then set off and stir into it a few ounces of pulverized Sugar, and flavor with Mint Oil; now, with a funnel dropper, run the Cream into drops on sheets of tin, the size of a silver quarter; in a few moments they will be dry and may be slid off the tins easily by turning them sidewise and bending once or twice backward and forward; they may also be run in starch prints if desired.

CREAM WINTERGREENS.

Same as Peppermint, except color Pink and flavor Wintergreen.

SMALL MINT DROPS.

Cook five pounds of Sugar, nearly a quart of water, and a small spoon of cream tartar, or one pound of glucose, to a Soft Ball; then set off near the fire to keep warm; pour a small quantity of the syrup into a lip pan, say a pint; add to it two or three tablespoons of pulverized Sugar; stir until it turns whiteish; then drop in small drops about the size of a dime on sheets of tin; cut the drops from the lip pan by means of a wire; if the Cream gets too thick to run easily, add some more syrup, and so continue until all the boiled Sugar is used up.

MOLASSES MINT DROPS.

Ten pounds of Sugar, water to dissolve, and a small spoon of cream tartar, or seven pounds of Sugar and three of glucose; when it boils, add one pint of New Orleans Molasses, and cook to a Hard Crack; pour out on a slab; when cold enough, pull all but about two pounds to a bright golden color; form it into a roll and stripe with the clear piece, as for stick candy; then spin out and mark with Caramel marker.

MINT CAKES.

Cook a batch same as for Mint Stick Candy; spin out about one inch in diameter, and cut with the shears into pieces about one inch in length; then stand them on end, and by placing the thumb on the top, press them into flat, round cakes; or, if making in large quantities, cut with a Jackson Ball cutter, and have two boards fastened together at one end with hinges; place a number of these cuts on end between the boards, and press them into cakes.

MINT KISSES.

Make a batch the same as for Cakes, but run it through a sour drop cutter.

LEMON CAKES.

Same as Mint, except leave the batch clear; place on it a white stripe, as in Lemon Stick Candy.

BOSTON CHIPS.

This Candy is very popular, but it requires considerable skill to make, so do not be disappointed if at your first trial you fail to get it perfect.

Take ten pounds of Sugar and a small spoon of cream tartar; use no glucose, as nicer goods in this line can be made with cream tartar; when it boils, add one-half pint New Orleans Molasses, and cook to 325°; pour on the slab, and when cold enough pull to a bright yellow; now, place it before the heater, and having a pair of gloves on, rub it on two sides until it assumes the appearance of satin; then spin it out into a thin, flat strip, rubbing it all the time, and let another person feed it through a Flake Machine; it will still retain its gloss; if you have no machine, it can be run out with the hands.

FLAKE CANDIES.

These candies are made in the same way as Boston Chips, either in white, red, or yellow.

STRINGS OF COMFORT.

Cook five pounds of Sugar and small spoon of cream tartar till the Sugar begins to turn, or about 330°; then pour out and pull perfectly white, and flavor cinnamon; form into a roll and spin out into strings about the thickness of a straw; while yet warm, curl them into different forms; when all is spun out, heap them on a pan; there can be several varieties of these made, coloring and flavoring to suit the taste.

PAN CREAMS.

Cook six pounds of Sugar, one quart of water, and a small spoon of cream tartar to a soft ball; set the batch away till nearly cold, then add a little Orange Flower water; stir until it turns whitish, then pour out in a Caramel pan; let it remain until cold; then turn the pan upside down, so the Cream will drop from the pan; mark it with a sharp knife into small squares; they may then be broken up.

Several flavors and colors of these Creams can be made in the same manner as above.

BUTTER SCOTCH.

Six pounds of Sugar, one-half pint Molasses and one spoon of cream tartar, or two pounds of glucose; when it begins to cook, add one-half pound of sweet Butter; stir until it reaches the crack, or 260°; add a few drops of Lemon Oil, and pour out on the slab between iron bars; mark into squares whatever size wished.

MAPLE CREAM FOR COUNTER.

Ten pounds of Maple Sugar, small spoon of cream tartar, and three pints of water; cook to a soft ball; set away till it is almost cold; then with the spatula cream it in the basin; as soon as it looks cloudy, pour it out at once in a deep pan; this must be done quickly or it will become hard in the basin; when cold, remove it from the pan in the same manner as the pan creams; mark it into bars or large squares for the counter.

CREAM BARS OR BABY CREAM.

Twelve pounds of Sugar, a small spoon of cream tartar, or one pound of glucose, two quarts of water; when it boils add two Vanilla Beans; cook to a Soft Crack, and pour out on a cold slab; pull until perfectly white; add a drop or so of Indigo on the hook, this will assist in whitening it; Sugar a warm slab by sieving over it pulverized Sugar; place the batch on one corner of the slab, and pull it out into strips the length of the slab; sieve Sugar over the strips; now, take an iron bar, one person being on the opposite side of the slab; press one edge of the iron bar across the strips, marking them into bars three or four inches in length; let it remain on the slab ten or twelve hours or until granulation takes place. Several varieties can be made, according to the flavor used—such as Mint, Cinnamon, Chocolate, etc. This candy can also be run through a drop machine, and in a day or so the drops will become creamy, and are very nice.

FIG BAR.

Twenty pounds of Sugar, or the same amount of Crystal Syrup; place it on the fire; when it reaches a thread, add ten pounds of Figs; cut up with the candy shears, or, what is better, grate them in the Cocoanut grater; stir until the batch reaches a large thread; set it off on a barrel, and sieve into it a pound or so of pulverized Sugar; then with the spatula work it on the sides of the basin until it becomes a thick mass; then pour out on a Sugared slab between iron bars; spread it of even thickness; now, dissolve eight or ten pounds of plain Cream in a basin inside of another basin containing water; color pink, and flavor nectar; pour this Cream over the Fig paste, and with a palette knife spread it evenly over the batch; leave it lay a few hours or over night; then cut it into bars or squares.

FIG PASTE.

Eight pounds of Sugar, two pounds of glucose, one pound and four ounces of Starch, two gallons of water, and a little less than one-half a teaspoon of dissolved Citric Acid; put the Sugar and water on the fire; add the acid; when the batch comes to a boil, add the starch dissolved in a little water; add whatever color, and flavor desired, and cook, stirring all the time, until by testing it in cold water, it leaves the fingers on cooling; pour it on a greased slab between iron bars; when cold, sieve over it pulverized Sugar, and cut it into small squares.

JELLY GUM DROPS—LEMON.

Twelve pounds of Sugar, two quarts of water, and a small spoon of cream tartar; put on the fire and dissolve; then add one pound of dissolved Gum Arabic, and a few drops of Lemon Oil; cook to a Soft Ball; then remove and with a funnel run it into starch prints; sieve a little starch powder over the tops, and set them in the dry closet till next day; then take them out of the starch, and crystalize or dip them in melted Fondant.

JELLY GUM DROPS—ROSE.

Same as Lemon, except color with a few drops of liquid Carmine, and flavor extract of Rose.

A. B. GUM DROPS—"OLD STYLE."

Put six pounds of pure white Gum Arabic into a basin with one-half gallon water; place this basin inside of another one containing water; put on the fire and stir until dissolved; then set off, and put on the fire ten pounds Sugar and cook to a good Soft Ball, and pour it into the dissolved Gum Arabic; now, let it remain undisturbed for awhile; a scum will form on the top; remove this, then with a funnel run it into starch prints; sieve some starch over the tops; put them into the closet at a temperature of about 150°; let remain until next day; then remove and dust off any loose starch with a fine brush, and put to crystal. If a hard Gum Drop is wanted, use more Gum Arabic and less Sugar.

CORDIAL DROPS.

Six pounds of Sugar, one quart water; cook a good thread, or about 222°; remove from the fire and add one pint of Cologne Spirits, or ninety-eight per cent. Alcohol, having added to it whatever color and flavor desired; now, with a funnel run it into starch prints; sieve a little starch powder over the tops, and set in the warm closet till next day, they may then be removed from the starch and crystalized or dipped in melted fondant. Brandy drops are made in the same manner, except use Brandy instead of Alcohol.

MARSHMALLOW DROPS.

Put into a basin five pounds of white Gum Arabic pulverized; add one-half gallon water; place this basin inside of another one containing water; set on the fire and stir till dissolved; then add nine pounds of pulverized Sugar, and evaporate until of a thick consistency; now, add the whites of two dozen Eggs; beat to a staunch foam, and stir until perfectly white and of a good body; or, until when laying the back of your hand on the batch, it does not adhere to it; flavor Orange Oil, Orange Flower water, or Vanilla; set off, and having a wide-mouthed bag with a tin spout, fill it with the mixture; hold in the left hand, and with the right cut the drops off with a small wire into starch prints; sieve a little starch powder over the tops, and set away in the closet till next day; they may then be removed and put into tin boxes; some use a decoction of Marshmallow Root in making the drops, but as it gives them a bitter taste, I always omit it.

GLACE NUTS AND FRUITS.

Select a small quantity of English Walnut halves, Brazil nuts, Cocoanut; cut into small squares, Cherries, Limes, Apricots, Pine Apple, both red and white; cut into small squares, Dates and Figs; spread all these out on a tray to dry, except the Cocoanut, which prepare in the following manner: Take three pounds of Sugar with one pint of water; when it boils, add the fresh Cocoanut, say, one whole one cut into small squares; cook just to a thread; remove and, with the spatula, work the syrup on the sides of the basin till it becomes cloudy; pour all on a wire sieve, having a pan under it to catch the syrup that drains from the Cocoanuts; set them away until dry. When ready to glace, cook six pounds of Sugar, a teaspoon of cream tartar, and one quart water to about 280 or 290°; pour it into a deep pan, having placed it on the center of a slab, on a rest of some kind, so the cold slab will not chill the syrup; now, throw into the syrup the Nuts and Fruits, one piece at a time, removing them with a dipping ladle and dropping them on the slab. Many other Fruits may be prepared in this way, and are very popular, such as Orange Slices, Malaga and California Grapes, etc., but only small quantities should be made at a time, as they soon become sticky when exposed to the atmosphere.

CREAM GOODS.

CREAM, OR FONDANT.

Particular attention must be given to the manufacture of Cream, as it is the basis of all Cream goods. Take twenty pounds of Sugar, three quarts of water, and two small teaspoons of cream of tartar or four pounds of glucose; put on the fire and stir until dissolved; cook to a Soft Ball then pour out on a marble slab, having previously been sprinkled with a little water; let it remain until cold, or nearly so; then turn in the edges, and with a long-handled wooden spatula or cream scraper, work it back and forward until it granulates into a smooth, white mass; now, knead it thoroughly with the hands and put it into a crock; cover with a damp cloth, and it is ready for such goods as plain and fancy Creams, Chocolate Cream Drops, Cream Walnuts, Figs, Dates, etc., etc.

FONDANT FOR DIPPING.

Use the same proportion of Sugar, water, cream of tartar, or glucose, as in previous batch; cook to the blow, or 230° strong; pour out on a cold, damp slab; let remain until perfectly cold, then cream as directed before. This Cream is used for all Dipped goods, Icing goods, etc.

HOW TO FLAVOR AND COLOR CREAM.

If Vanilla flavor is wished, add when the batch begins to boil one Vanilla Bean to each seven pounds of Sugar; prepare the Beans in the following manner: Split them in halves to the stem; scrape out the centers; place these on the slab so they may be incorporated in the syrup; while creaming the Beans, add to the batch; or, if flavoring with extract, pour it on the batch while on the slab; the color should be added when the batch reaches the boiling point.

SYRUP FOR CRYSTALIZING.

Take any number pounds of Sugar, one quart of water to each six pounds, and boil to 34° by the saccharometer if a fine crystal is desired; if a coarse one, boil to 36°; set off and let remain undisturbed until nearly or quite cold; then sprinkle a little water over it to dissolve the thin crystal coating that has formed over the top; it is now ready for use; having placed the goods for crystalizing in pans, with a dipper pour the syrup carefully over them until covered; then place over each pan damp cloths, allowing them to rest on the syrup, this takes up the crust of Sugar that forms on top of the syrup; set the pans where they will be undisturbed for about eight or nine hours; then place them in the crystal trough; drain off the syrup and let remain until dry; remove the cloths from them; turn the pans upside down on a table, and the goods will fall out.

CASTING IN STARCH.

This process consists in having a number of starched trays, which are made of wood about two and one-half or three feet in length, eighteen or twenty inches in width, and two inches in depth; fill these with fine, dry starch powder and level the top; now, with plaster molds, which are made fast to a strip of wood one or two inches wide, according to the size of the molds, press into the starch and remove carefully; take a Confectioner's funnel and a round stick which just fits the small hole at the bottom of the funnel, and long enough to give a hand hold above the funnel; fill part full with syrup, and holding it over the starch prints raise the stick a little and allow enough syrup to escape to fill the print, and so on till all are filled; then remove to the starch closet; when they have remained long enough sieve off the starch; if there is still some starch adhering, dust it off with a fine brush; then place the goods in pans for crystalizing.

MAPLE FONDANT.

It is made in the same manner as other Cream, except use Maple Sugar instead of Confectioner's A, and a little less cream of tartar or glucose; if wished to tone down the strong flavor of the Maple, use one half Maple and one-half Confectioner's A.

DIPPED BONBONS.

Take three or four pounds of Cream made for dipping; put it into a porcelain dipper enclosed in a jacket containing water; place this on the fire, and when the water boils, set off and stir and work the Cream with a small spatula until it is the consistency of Milk Cream; now, place the dipping pot on a table; arrange the centers to be dipped on the left of the pot, and a clean sheet of tin on the right; drop a center in the Cream; then with a wire ladle or an ordinary fork, dip the center, and removing it, drop it on the sheet of tin; in a little while they will be hard enough to handle. In this mixture dip English Walnut halves, Pineapple cut into squares, whole Cherries, in this case; color the Cream pink and flavor Nectar; Marshmallow Drops making the Cream any color desired; Almond paste formed into small balls; color the Cream a green tint; Quince Jelly, Cream colored Orange tint; Citron cut into squares, Cream, white and Vanilla flavor; Nougat cut into small strips, chopped-up Black Walnuts, chopped Pistache Nuts, Filberts, Brazil Nuts, Cocoanut, etc.

CORDIALS DIPPED.

Dip Cordial Drops in this same Fondant as mentioned above; they are very nice and popular in the winter season, but do not stand well in summer.

DIPPED MAPLE BONBONS.

Prepare three or four pounds of Maple Cream in the same manner as for white and for centers; cook two pounds of Maple Sugar to a Soft Ball, and whip into it the whites of three Eggs; beat to a staunch foam; when cold, roll into balls and dip; also dip English Walnut halves in this Cream. Another nice center for Maple is one fresh grated Cocoanut, and one and one-half pounds of pulverized Sugar worked into a paste, rolled into balls and dipped. Still another: Cook four pounds of Maple Sugar with one spoon cream of tartar to 265°, and stir into it two grated Cocoanuts; pour out on a damp slab, cream it and form it into balls.

CHOCOLATE BONBONS.

Put into a dipping-pot one ounce of Chocolate to each pound of Cream to be used; place the pot on the fire, and when the Chocolate is melted, add the Cream and stir it until dissolved; add about one-fourth of a pint of simple syrup to each pound of melted Fondant; this is now ready for dipping; use for centers, English Walnuts, Hickory-nuts, or Brazil Nuts; chop them very fine, and work sufficient Cream with them to form a paste. A Chocolate center made in the following way is very nice: Cook to a Soft Ball three pounds of Sugar, a half spoon cream tartar, and three ounces of Chocolate; set off and stir into it one-fourth ounce ground cinnamon; granulate a moment, then with a funnel run them into starch prints, any style desired; set them in the closet; next day they may be removed from the starch and dipped.

CONSERVE BONBONS.

Cook four pounds of Sugar, a little more than one pint of water, and a small spoon of cream tartar to a Soft Ball; set off and add two or three tablespoons of pulverized Sugar; then, with a small wooden spatula, work the Sugar on the sides of the basin till it becomes whitish; then pour into the dipping-pot, having the water in the jacket boiling; color and flavor any shade or flavor wished, and dip any kind of Jelly centers, dropping them on sheets of tin; when cold, with a small brush dipped in any color wanted, touch the tops of all the Bonbons. For example, if the Bonbons are pink, use red color.

DIPPED JELLY GUMS.

Dip Fresh Jelly Gum Drops in melted Fondant, and drop them into a pan or tray containing chopped-up Walnuts, or any nuts desired; roll into balls and crystallize.

COCOANUT MARSHMALLOW BONBONS.

Cut fresh Marshmallow Drops into four pieces each, and dip them in melted Fondant, pink color, Rose or Nectar flavor, and drop them into a pan containing grated Cocoanut; prepare the Cocoanut in the following manner: Take white desiccated Cocoanut; sieve it, rejecting all the fine siftings; pour on the remainder a few drops of red color; stir them thoroughly until all are a pink shade; roll the dipped drops in this, and when cold, arrange them in pans for crystallizing.

FRUIT ICINGS.

Take of dipping Cream any number of pounds desired, say five; put it into a basin inside of another one containing water; place on the fire; stir the Cream until dissolved, but not thin; add a few drops of red color, and flavor Nectar or Strawberry; pour this into a starch tray, lined with good strong Manilla paper; spread it in a thin layer over the bottom; now, put over the fire in the same way eight pounds of Cream, and dissolve as before; stir into this three or four pounds of Cherries, Pineapple, Citron and Apricots, cut up; pour this on top of the first layer, and spread of even thickness; now, again melt five pounds of Cream, color a bright green, and pour on top of this last; set away until next day, then turn the tray upside down on a table, and the Cream will drop out; remove the paper and run a Caramel marker over it two ways, and cut it into squares and crystallize.

ALMOND ICINGS.

Use of same Cream as before, about five pounds; dissolve, and pour it into a tray; now, melt one-half pound of Chocolate in the basin, and add eight pounds of Cream; dissolve and stir in three pounds of Almond Nuts; pour on first layer and spread of even thickness; then again, melt of white Cream five pounds, and spread it over the last, finish as before.

HICKORY-NUT ICINGS.

Take ten pounds of same Cream as used before; place it in a basin and dissolve as before; stir in three pounds of choice Hickory-nuts, and pour out in a tray, spreading of even thickness; when cold, mark with Caramel marker, and crystalize or cook ten pounds of Sugar, three pints of water, one teaspoon of cream tartar to a Strong Ball; let it stand awhile to become cool; then whip into it the whites of four Eggs beat to a staunch foam; when it is pure white stir in three pounds of Hickory-nuts, and pour into a tray, and spread of even thickness; finish as before. A great many varieties of these goods can be made in this manner, combining different flavors and colors to suit taste.

FRUIT NOUGAT.

Dissolve as for Fruit Icings ten pounds of Cream; whip into it the whites of three or four Eggs; then stir in three pounds of French Fruits, such as Pineapple, red and white, Plums, Cherries, etc.; pour into a deep pan and set away till next day; then cut into large squares, same as Nougat, and wrap in wax paper.

CREAM WALNUTS.

Roll with the hands a piece of Cream into a strip about one inch in diameter; then with a knife cut into pieces about one inch in length; roll into a ball, and place a Walnut half on two sides opposite each other; place them in pans, and when they have stood a few hours, they may be crystallized. Another way, form on a slab a cone of sifted pulverized Sugar; any number of pounds desired; hollow out the top and pour in a small quantity at a time of any pure Fruit juice; work it into a stiff Cream, and color whatever shade corresponds to the flavor used; then roll out and serve in the same manner as before; these are very popular and handsome made in such colors as white, red, yellow, orange and green; crystallize as before.

CREAM DATES.

Select choice whole dates; press with the fingers the seed to one side, and with a pair of shears cut the date in half lengthwise; the seed can now be removed without spoiling the appearance of the date; fill them with Cream and roll them in the hands lengthwise, making them long and slim; place them in pans and crystallize. Made in this way, they are very handsome; they may be made in white, red, yellow, orange and green.

CREAM CHERRIES AND RAISINS.

Select only nice, large Fruit, and open one-half of them and fill with smooth Cream any color or flavor desired—Vanilla being the most popular.

CREAM BONBONS.

Having filled a number of starch trays with fine dry starch, print any design desired; then put into a basin four or five pounds of Fondant; place this inside of another basin containing water and set on the fire; when dissolved, color and flavor as desired; then remove from the basin containing water, and set over the fire a moment, stirring all the time; do not let it come to a boil, as that would change it into a conserve when cold; now, with a funnel, run it into the prints and set in the closet till next day; then take them out on a sieve; dust off any adhering starch with a fine brush or bellows, they are now ready for crystallizing.

JELLY CREAM BONBONS.

Make impressions in the starch trays with molds having two separate designs, one smaller than the other; now make a Jelly from Apples, color and flavor it to suit taste; then run it into the lowest impression in the starch; after filling all, and they have become cold, dissolve a quantity of Fondant to the consistency of Cream; color and flavor; now, with the funnel, fill the impressions full over the Jelly; set in the closet, and in a few hours they may be taken out, placed in a sieve, and dusted; then put into pan for crystallizing. These molds, having separate designs, may be filled with different colored Cream, and they look very handsome.

CONSERVE BONBONS.

Print a few starch trays with whatever designs wished; cook five pounds of Sugar, a small spoon of cream tartar, and one quart of water to a Soft Ball; set off and stir in one pound of soft dipping Cream; color and flavor; then with a small wooden spatula rub the syrup on the sides of the basin until it assumes a whitish appearance; pour a portion of it into a funnel, setting the remainder near the fire to keep warm; run into the starch prints; in a little while they may be removed, dusted and put to crystal.

CONSERVE ICINGS.

Cook a batch in the same way as for Conserve Bonbons; whip into it the whites of two Eggs, and, when done, instead of running in starch, stir in two pounds of Hickory-nuts or any nuts desired; pour in a tray lined with paper; as soon as cold, cut into squares and crystallize. Several varieties of these Icings can be made, and they are delicious.

LOG ICINGS.

Chop up a few pounds of blanched Almonds; sieve them, rejecting the siftings; divide the remainder into three equal parts; now, take one lot and putting it into a bowl, pour on a few drops of red color; work them with a spatula until all are colored; then spread them out on a sheet of paper to dry; treat the second lot in the same way, coloring it yellow; then the third, coloring it green; now, take of desiccated Cocoanut the same amount; sieve and color red, yellow and green; color and flavor a quantity of Fondant red, yellow, orange and chocolate; take of the chocolate one-half pound; form into a roll; now, take of the yellow double the quantity; form it into a sheet just reaching around the chocolate; then put a green sheet around this, and with the hands roll it out into a strip one inch in diameter, and cut them into pieces about twelve inches in length; lay these on sheets of tin, or a tray, to harden a little; when firm enough to keep their shape, pour a little simple syrup on a slab; roll a strip in the syrup, then again in any of the colored nuts, and lay aside until the nuts adhere firmly to the Cream; then cut into pieces diagonally, about one inch in length; proceed in the same way with all the Cream, forming it into rolls, combining such colors as suit the taste, and rolling them in the different colored nuts and combinations of nuts; roll some of the strips in melted chocolate, then again in the nuts; these goods are unequalled for dressing fancy boxes.

ACORN BONBONS.

Color a number of pounds of Almond Paste a bright green, and roll out into strips; cut into pieces of equal size; then form into round drops, having one end shaped pointed like an Acorn; when all the paste is formed in this way, prepare a Chocolate Fondant, same as for dipping Chocolate Bonbons. Sieve a quantity of A Sugar, reserving only the large bright crystals; put this into a pan; now, take an Acorn in the hand and dip the blunt end in the Fondant; then stand it in the Sugar, Chocolate end down, so on drying small crystals of Sugar will be adhering to the cap; continue in this manner till all are done; then arrange them in pans and crystallize.

FIG CREAMS.

Take green Figs preserved; cut them into quarters, leaving them connected at the stem; now, prepare a quantity of Cream, colored pink, and flavored strawberry, nectar or rose; roll into a strip, cut into pieces of equal size; form them in cones; put one of these inside of each Fig, the base next the stem; press the quarters against the Cream; then with a fine brush dipped in red color; make four stripes on each one, starting at the base of the Fig between each quarter, and running to the point of the Cream; place in pans and crystallize.

JELLY ROLLS.

Cook a stiff Apple Jelly, color red, and flavor rose or any other flavor desired; spread it out on a greased slab, and when cold lay it on a sheet of Cream of same thickness, roll up, cut into slices and crystallize.

ALMOND CONFITS.

Select a quantity of whole Dates; press the seed to one side and cut them in halves lengthwise; remove the seed and put a Jordan Almond inside; close together again and dip in melted Fondant, and when cold, cut them in halves and crystallize.

CRAB APPLES.

Take of white Cream two or three pounds; same amount of red, yellow and chocolate; form these into strips triangle in shape; place them together in such a way as to form a Round Roll; now, with the hands roll out into a strip about one inch in diameter, and cut into pieces of equal size; roll again into balls; then with a sharp stick make indentations on the two ends of each; arrange in pans and crystallize.

PINEAPPLE CREAMS.

Cut a quantity of Pineapple into small, narrow strips; roll out with a rolling-pin a sheet of Cream quite thin; any color, and with a tin tube one inch in diameter, cut a number of cakes; lay a strip of Pineapple on each cake, and fold two sides together over the strips. A very small ribbon may be tied around this and then put to crystal.

A great many more fancy hand-made designs might be mentioned, but a sufficient amount have been already named to give any one an idea of how to get them up, and if, after becoming familiar with the modus operandi as given in this volume, they possess some originality, their imagination will readily assist them in producing new designs to the already large variety.

CHOCOLATE WORK.

HOW TO MAKE CHOCOLATE CREAM DROPS.

The first thing needed is a Chocolate warmer; this consists in a large tin or sheet-iron pan, inside of which is a smaller one arranged so water can circulate between them; set this pan on the fire, and bring the water to a boil; set off and put into the warmer any quantity desired of sweet Chocolate, having pounded it fine, so as to melt readily; stir thoroughly until dissolved into a thin paste; add a little ground cinnamon; now, having prepared the drops for dipping, in the following manner, viz.: Roll out a piece of Cream into a strip; then with a knife cut it into pieces of equal size; roll it again into balls; lay them in trays until they have dried a little, so they will keep their shape; then pour a cup of melted Chocolate on the warm slab (this should be a small marble slab, set in a frame, having an oil or gas stove, or a few gas jets under it; heat this slab blood warm); throw into it a number of these Cream Balls; work them around in the Chocolate until coated; then drop them from the hand with the forefinger and thumb on sheets of tin covered with wax paper; set them in a cool place until the Chocolate hardens; they are then ready for use; in summer they should be put into an ice chest until hardened.

Another way to prepare the Cream for dipping, is to dissolve a few pounds of Cream in the same manner as for Bonbons; then with a funnel run it into starch prints; in a little while they may be removed from the starch, dusted and dipped as before. In this same mixture may be dipped drops made from powdered Sugar in the following way: Grate the outside rine of a few Lemons, and having formed the Sugar into a cone, hollow out the top; pour into this the juice squeezed from the Lemons, together with the rine, and work all into a Cream; do the same with Oranges and with any kind of Fruit juice; add a little Citric Acid dissolved in water to bring out the Fruit flavor; also, dip in this mixture roasted Almonds, Nougat cut into small squares, Marshmallow Drops, Cocoanut Paste, plain Fondant squares, placing an English Walnut half on the top.

TO MAKE SWEET CHOCOLATE FROM PLAIN.

Melt in the Chocolate warmer any number pounds of Cocoa Paste; when dissolved stir into it one half pound of fine Sugar dust to each pound of Cocoa Paste.

PRALINES OR FANCY CHOCOLATES.

Cook four pounds of Sugar, small spoon of cream tartar, one quart rich Cream to a very soft ball; set off and work the Sugar on the sides of the basin with a small wooden spatula until it turns cloudy; work this cloud into the body of the Sugar, and so on until it has a whitish appearance throughout; then, with a funnel, run it into starch prints; in a few hours they may be taken out, dusted and dipped in melted Chocolate, in the same manner as Bonbons, with a wire ladle, dropping them on sheets of tin covered with wax paper; make them in Vanilla, Strawberry, Nectar, Lemon, Orange and Coffee. To make Coffee, take one-half pound best ground Coffee to one quart of water; set on the fire and bring to a boil; set off and let simmer a few moments; then strain, and use this liquid to cook the Sugar with instead of Cream, and finish as before; any kind of Jelly may be dipped in Chocolate, and are very nice.

To thin Chocolate when too thick for dipping, add a little Cocoa Butter, Rape Seed Oil or fresh melted Suet.

To thicken when too thin, add fine Sugar dust. Chocolate for dipping can be flavored with vanilla sugar, ground cinnamon, cloves, allspice or mace.

VARNISH FOR CHOCOLATE WORK.

Place in a glass jar a quantity of Gum Shellac; pour over it enough Alcohol to cover; let remain till next day; when ready to use, pour out a quantity in a vessel; add Alcohol until of the consistency of varnish, then apply with a brush.

APPLE JELLY.

Take any quantity of Sweet Apples; cut them into slices, and put them into a basin with enough water to cover; set on the fire and cook until quite soft; remove and rub through a fine sieve; now, if wishing to run this in starch for dipping, add to one quart of this pulp one ounce of dissolved Gelatine; then cook five pounds of Sugar to a Good Ball, and stir in this pulp; now, with a funnel, run it into the starch prints; next day, after removing them from the starch and dusting, they are ready to dip; but if a stiff Jelly is wanted for Jelly Rolls, etc., add to each pint of this pulp one pound of pulverized Sugar; set on the fire and boil, stirring all the time, until it begins to adhere to the spatula; then remove and pour out into pans or trays, spreading it of any thickness wished; this is the basis of almost all Jellies, such as Strawberry, Raspberry, Pineapple, etc.; simply color and flavor to to suit taste.

APRICOT JELLY.

Cook ten pounds of Sugar to a Hard Ball; then add to it five pounds of Apricot Pulp, having strained it through a fine sieve; pour a portion into a funnel and set the rest near the fire to keep warm; run it into starch prints, and let it remain until next day: they may then be removed, dusted free of any adhering starch, and dipped in melted Fondant.

PRESERVING FRUITS.

Select the finest Fruit, but not too ripe, and pare such as Peaches, Quinces and Pears; then, with an ordinary fork, prick them to the seed in several places, so that the air in the Fruit may escape, and also so the Sugar may enter the Fruit more easily; as they are pricked throw them into cold water, this prevents them from becoming black in the places pricked; now, put them into a basin of hot water, letting them simmer until parboiled, then, with a skimming ladle, dip them from the hot water and drop them into a basin of cold water, allowing them to remain a few moments; remove from the water and put on a hair sieve to drain; when drained, put them in a wide-mouthed crock and bring to a boil a quantity of simple syrup; pour this over the Fruit; then place a plate over the top to hold the Fruit under the syrup; set away till next day, then empty this crock of Fruit and put the syrup again into the basin, and bring just to the boil; return again to the crock and cover with the plate; do this each following day, for six days; by this time the Fruit will take up no more Sugar; put them into a cool place.

GLAZED FRUITS.

Cook a few pounds of Sugar to a blow; set off and add such preserved Fruits as are wanted; then, with a small wooden spatula, work the Sugar against the sides of the basin until cloudy; now, dip out the Fruits with a skimming ladle, placing them on a wire screen to dry, which will require an hour or so; they are then ready for the counter.

BRANDIED CHERRIES.

Take an open mouthed jar, till it part full of simple Syrup, adding to it Alcohol until of such strength as desired, and put into this a quantity of preserved Cherries. When they have received sufficient flavor to suit taste, they may be removed and dipped in melted Fondant.

SYRUPS FOR THE SODA-WATER FOUNTAIN.

As nearly two-thirds of the Confectioners handle Soda-Water, a few practical receipts for making the Syrups most used, will, I think, be acceptable to many.

In preparing Syrups for the Fountain use only the best Confectioner's A Sugar, as this renders the Syrups transparent; does not decompose so readily, and saves the time and trouble of clarification, which is necessary if a poor quality of Sugar is used.

Syrups are best preserved by putting them in small earthern jugs, well corked, and in a cool place, ranging in temperature from 40 to 50° Fahr. To prevent Syrups from granulating, add a small teaspoon of cream of tartar to each twelve and a half pounds of Sugar. Syrups that have fermented may be restored again by bringing them to the boiling point. Always use a copper basin in preparing all Fruit Syrups.

SIMPLE SYRUP.

To each gallon of water add one-fourth ounce Gelatine; stir until dissolved, then add twelve and a half pounds of Confectioner's A Sugar; stir until dissolved; set off and remove the scum and place in an earthern jug for use as needed. A variety of Syrups may be made from this Syrup by adding flavoring and color; but they are artificial at best, and do not compare with those made from Fruit juices.

VANILLA SYRUP.

Split three Vanilla Beans and scrape out the centers; add the Beans together with the centers to one gallon of water and one-fourth ounce Gelatine; allow to boil a few moments; then add twelve and one-half pounds best Sugar; stir until all is dissolved; remove and take off the scum and strain into a jug. A very good Vanilla Syrup may be made by adding to simple Syrup about five ounces of Vanilla extract to each gallon.

CHOCOLATE SYRUP.

Place on the fire one gallon of water; when it boils, add twelve ounces of Chocolate pounded fine; stir until dissolved, then remove and let stand until nearly cold; when a scum of grease will form on the top, remove this and set again on the fire, and add twelve and one-half pounds best Sugar; stir until dissolved; set off and strain into a jug. Many do not skim off the grease, thinking a better Chocolate flavor is obtained by placing all in an open-mouthed crock or jar, and stirring this scum into the body of the Syrup each time before using; but I prefer the former.

COFFEE SYRUP.

To one pound of pure roasted and ground Java Coffee add one gallon water; place on the fire, and when it boils, remove and cover, allowing it to remain so until nearly cold; then strain, and having placed the decoction again on the fire, add twelve and one-half pounds Sugar; stir until all has dissolved and reached the temperature of boiling; set off and strain into a jug.

LEMON SYRUP.

To one gallon simple Syrup add one-half ounce of dissolved Citric Acid (dissolve the Acid by adding one pound of water to one pound of Acid), and a sufficient amount of fresh Lemon Oil to suit taste.

Another Formula.—Take the grated yellow rinds of any quantity of fresh Lemons; place them in a closed vessel in the proportion of one pint of boiling water to each six Lemons; let remain a few hours, then strain; now, press the juice from all the Lemons grated, and add this to the juice from the gratings, and to each pint of this add one pint of water and three and one-half pounds of Sugar; place on the fire and stir until dissolved; do not let it boil; set off and strain into a jug.

ORANGE SYRUP.

Proceed in the same manner as for Lemon Syrup, using the grated yellow rinds of fresh Oranges, or flavor simple Syrup with extract Orange, adding one-half ounce dissolved Citric Acid to each gallon, and color with saffron and a few drops carmine.

STRAWBERRY SYRUP.

To three quarts water; having dissolved in it one-fourth ounce Gelatine, add one quart pure Strawberry juice; place on the fire and add a small quantity of carmine to color; now, add twelve and one-half pounds Sugar; stir until dissolved; remove and take off the scum, then add one-half ounce dissolved Citric Acid; strain into a jug and when cold cork well.

Raspberry, Blackberry, Pineapple and *Cherry* are all made in the same manner.

PEACH AND APRICOT.

Take a quantity of ripe Peaches or Apricots; remove the stones; place them on the fire, and adding to them water in the proportion of one quart to four quarts of Peaches; stir all the time until reduced to a pulp; pour into a crock, and when cold, strain through a fine sieve; then, having dissolved one-fourth ounce of Gelatine in three quarts of water, add one quart of the above juice, and twelve and one-half pounds of Sugar, and finish as Strawberry, etc.

NECTAR SYRUP.

Flavor simple Syrup to suit taste with extract Nectar, and color pink, with a few drops of Carmine or Cochineal.

ANOTHER FORMULA.—Thoroughly mix together three pints of Vanilla Syrup with one pint of Pineapple and one of Lemon; this forms a very nice Nectar.

CATAWBA SYRUP.

Add to simple Syrup, colored a delicate pink with Carmine, a sufficient quantity of extract Catawba to suit taste.

ANOTHER FORMULA.—To one quart simple Syrup add one quart of Catawba Wine; this forms a delicious Syrup.

ORGEAT OR ALMOND SYRUP.

To one and a half pounds of fresh blanched sweet Almonds add one or two ounces of bitter ones; pound these to a smooth paste in a mortar; then add one pint of water and mix; place this mixture in a towel, and twist from it all the milk possible; to this milk add three pounds pulverized Sugar; dissolve cold, and add a small quantity of Orange Flower water; strain into a closed jar, and shake often to keep the milk from separating from the Sugar.

GINGER SYRUP.

Color one gallon simple Syrup with a little burnt Sugar, and add to it one-half ounce Tartaric Acid, and two or three ounces essence Ginger to suit taste.

CREAM SYRUP.

This is prepared simply by adding fresh Cream to well-flavored Syrups.

SHERBERT SYRUP.

Take an equal proportion of Orange, Vanilla and Pineapple Syrups mixed.

SARSAPARILLA SYRUP.

Flavor simple Syrup to suit taste with extract Sarsaparilla, and color with burnt Sugar.

CAYENNE SYRUP.

Color pink one gallon simple Syrup, and add two ounces of tincture Capsicum, and mix well together.

CINNAMON SYRUP.

Flavor simple Syrup to suit taste with extract Cinnamon.

MAPLE SYRUP.

Place on the fire one quart of water, add one-fourth ounce Gelatine; when dissolved, add four pounds pure Maple Sugar; dissolve and strain in a jug.

Lector House believes that a society develops through a two-fold approach of continuous learning and adaptation, which is derived from the study of classic literary works spread across the historic timeline of literature records. Therefore, we aim at reviving, repairing and redeveloping all those inaccessible or damaged but historically as well as culturally important literature across subjects so that the future generations may have an opportunity to study and learn from past works to embark upon a journey of creating a better future.

This book is a result of an effort made by Lector House towards making a contribution to the preservation and repair of original ancient works which might hold historical significance to the approach of continuous learning across subjects.

HAPPY READING & LEARNING!

LECTOR HOUSE LLP
E-MAIL: lectorpublishing@gmail.com